Dedication:

This guidebook is dedicated to every person who bravely attempts new things, hungrily seeks to learn new tools, and who actively comes to the table desiring to make new friends. I welcome you to the social mix and am so excited that you are about to join the social conversation. This book is dedicated to you.

About the author:

Kathryn Rose is a Certified Social Media strategist and trainer, specializing in integration of new technologies in marketing strategies, Search Engine Optimization (SEO), Mobile Marketing and Social Media development and training to help clients maximize their visibility online. A featured speaker on New Technology Marketing at the Real Estate University, Ladies Who Launch, Loan Officer Magazine, and the International Social Media Association, Kathryn spent 15 years as a top marketing and sales professional in Residential Real Estate and Finance, most recently as top salesperson for Credit Suisse where she was responsible for over $100m per year in sales. Kathryn also developed the world's first mobile autoresponder, MobiReply, a cutting edge mobile marketing product which helps clients seamlessly integrate their current email marketing campaigns with a dynamic mobile marketing platform. Her 20-plus years in marketing, sales and public relations uniquely positions her to offer cross platform sales driving strategies to clients. Kathryn has helped countless entrepreneurs, small and large organizations utilize online and social media marketing for business retention and growth. Kathryn is the author of 6 books on social media for business: Step by Step Guides to Facebook, Twitter, Linkedin and SEO/Video for business as well as *The Parent's Guide to Facebook and the Grandparent's Guide to Facebook*.

Connect with Kathryn:

Facebook : http://facebook.com/katrose

Twitter: http://twitter.com/katkrose

Linkedin: http://linkedin.com/in/katkrose

About Contributor Tisho Richardson

Tisho Richardson is a Web Developer and Internet Marketing Expert with over 5 years of hands-on experience in the field of Internet Marketing. Currently Tisho is a freelance internet marketing consultant lending his expertise to authors, organizations and internet marketing experts worldwide. In addition to white paper solutions, Tisho's guidance and expertise has increased traffic and brand engagement to one of today's major players in the online dating advice niche as well as numerous startup and mid-level internet entities. He is also the genius behind the highly successful and informative internet marketing news site Newsfly411 http://newsfly411.com.

Tisho has spent the last 5 years honing his talents by participating in numerous information product launches and internet marketing events with some of the web's most brilliants minds. Tisho's professional skill set includes Web Analytics, Eye Movement analysis, Search Engine Optimization, PPC Marketing, CPA Marketing, Press Exposure and Social Media Optimization. Tisho takes pride in constantly educating himself in new technologies and the ever changing landscape that is today's internet.

Table of Contents

Chapter 1: Building Your Brand on the Internet

To get started I will cover a bit of the history of SEO, search engine optimization, how it started and why it's important.

What is search engine optimization? The internet has VAST amounts of information. How do you find what you want when you are searching? People don't want to do too much work when they want information, they want it now. Google came up with sophisticated algorithms called "spiders" that search the internet and determine which sites are more relevant than others in relation to certain "keywords." That is why when you type in "shoes" you don't get a site for real estate.

In the beginning, internet marketers used certain tactics to rank for all different kinds of keywords, non-relevant ones, in the hopes that they would get some leads. There was a backlash and the search engines took notice. They go to great pains to make sure that your results are RELEVANT. How do you become relevant? You need to build a brand or a "niche."

Why do you need to rank?

Here are some interesting statistics:

- **85% of people found information through search engines**
- **81% found new websites using search engines**
- **93% of people do not go past the second page of search engine results**

Because of the sheer volume of information and competitive websites available on the internet, it is more important than ever to carve out a niche for your brand. Most businesses try to be all things to all people and but with brand building you can stand out in the crowd. As you build your own brand, you will be able to compete better in your marketplace and carve out a niche of loyal clients.

To create or carve out a niche follow these simple steps:

- ➢ **do a search for your area of expertise in Google and yahoo—what sites come up?**
- ➢ **learn how people can and do search the search engines. Google cheat sheet http://www.Google.com/help/cheatsheet.html**
- ➢ **investigate little used niches—for example, instead of trying to rank for California Real Estate, try and to rank for your specific location in California, or further, market yourself as a "new home" expert or "waterfront properties" expert**
- ➢ **use Google keyword tool https://adwords.Google.com/select/KeywordToolExternal a free tool to investigate who is searching for different words and how many of them there are.**

Chapter 2: Keyword research

There are 3 main types of searches done on the internet

> **Navigational – Type your website name *i.e.* nytimes.com**
>
> **Informational – New York Newspaper**
>
> **Transactional - Buy New York Newspaper**

Free tools: Google keyword

https://adwords.Google.com/select/KeywordToolExternal

For brand-building and/or "niche" building—you don't have to have the masses come to your site -- you only need a few searchers that are SPECIFICALLY looking for what you offer.   Many businesses think they have to rank for broad terms such as "real estate" or "shoes". Unless you are a national shoe or real estate chain you will not need to rank for such broad terms.   For example, if your business only focuses on Stamford, CT real estate or

Children's shoes, that word (or words) is what you want to rank for.

It doesn't happen overnight, however. SEO takes time and needs to be targeted. If you want to rank quickly hire a good SEO firm. If 85% of your potential customers start their search on the internet, it would be a wise investment to make in the future of your business. Once you are consistently out there for at least a year, you may not have to keep paying the SEO firm, your site will need regular updates, but you can do some of that on your own.

Don't worry though, I'll give you plenty of free resources to help you rank on your own. This information will also be helpful so you can "talk the talk" to web developers and template website companies. They build pretty websites but they don't rank. I'll talk more about that in the next strategy…

Often times when I speak to clients about keyword

research I ask them to begin by writing down the top 50 keywords they think either people would type in the search bar to find them or they would LIKE to rank for.

This helps me and my team begin to dig in to find niche keyword terms that will help your website rank higher, faster. When you do this exercise, however, you will want to keep in mind what I said earlier. Don't write down "real estate" if you are only local to Phoenix, AZ.

Use this space to write down your top 50 keywords

_____

_____

_____

_____

_____

_____

Using Google Keyword Tool

Below are screenshots of the Google keyword tool. It is a free resource to give you an idea of who is searching for what keywords. Use the keywords you think your clients are using to search for you and then see what terms Google tells you they are really looking for. Your best bet? Find a keyword that has some regular traffic but not a lot of competition,--that will be a keyword you should target.

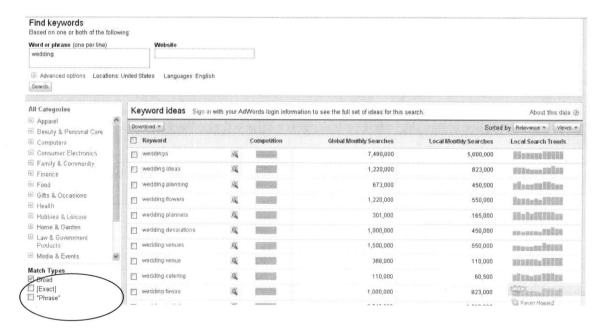

Keyword Matching Options

You can set each search-targeted keyword to have one of three settings: broad match, phrase match, or exact match. These three keyword matching options can help you narrow down the search terms you should incorporate into your SEO strategy.

To use a keyword matching option check the box next to one of the options. If you don't add any of the specified punctuation, your keyword will be broad match by default.

Here's a summary of the three options:

> Broad match: **keyword *(no punctuation)***
  Allows your ad to show for searches on similar phrases and relevant variations
> Exact match: **[keyword]**
  Allows your ad to show for searches that match the exact phrase exclusively

➢ Phrase match: **"keyword"**

Allows your ad to show for searches that match the exact phrase

I only use "phrase" or [exact] match. The reason for this is simple. Google returns results on page one that are the MOST RELEVANT. If your site ranks for exact or phrase you will be the most relevant in that category. These options give you the most relevant and appropriate keywords for your particular niche.

The **Local Search Trends** gives you a month by month graph of "trends" on that search term meaning what months does that search term get the most traffic.

Extra tip: The "long tail"—the long tail is an industry term that is used to describe how people search. For example, type in real estate and you get millions of searches or type in CT Real Estate, narrowing it down, then type in Fairfield County CT real estate and so forth. You would be wise not to ignore the "long tail" searchers—these people know what they want and may exactly be your target audience. Also, it's easier to rank for some of these terms initially so you may want to start there.

Now that you have researched your top 50 keywords, write down the number of monthly searches from the Google Keyword tool. Remember, you're looking for keywords that have a good number of monthly searches but not so many that you can see it would be a highly competitive keyword. You can see the "competition" bar next to each term on the Google Keyword tool. This shows how many people pay Google to advertise for that term. That is a good indicator of how competitive the keyword is. Remember, you want high monthly searches and low competition. If you see that all of your keywords have high competition, try to continue to narrow it down.

This is especially true if you are doing this on your own. You will want to try and keep it manageable by finding "niche" keywords.

Chapter 3: Local Search Engine Listings

Most of the top search engines offer a version of the local search and it's one of the fastest ways to get traffic and also one of the simplest.

You will want to have your keyword list handy and "Google search" Google Places. The link for this service is too long to include here.

Google places is a great way for small businesses to quickly rank their pizza shop or nail salon on Google. It is essentially the yellow pages of Google and if you use the right keywords, you can come up on the first page virtually overnight.

There are many advantages to signing up for Google Places:

> **Local listings often times come up first on search engines, see the following example :**

Google hairdresser fairfield ct [Search] Advanced Search

Web ⊞ Show options...   Results **1 - 10** of a

Local business results for **hairdresser** near **Fairfield, CT**

(A) hair
www.cthair.com - (203) 255-1041 - More

(B) Robert Christie Salon
www.robertchristiesalon.com - (203) 255-6668 - More

(C) D.Sabrina Salon
maps.google.com - (203) 256-8209 - More

(D) Hair Sculptures, LLC
maps.google.com - (203) 339-5838 - More

(E) Beautiful Faces
www.beautiful-faces.com - (203) 226-1818 - 1 review

(F) JoDavi.. the salon
www.jodavisalon.com - (203) 374-7111 - 2 reviews

As you can see by the arrow, you don't even need a
WEBSITE to come up here and you come up first in the
search!

> **Analytics—Google provides you with information on
> how many people saw your listing, how many click
> through to your website, etc. and also offers advice
> on how you can improve your listing**

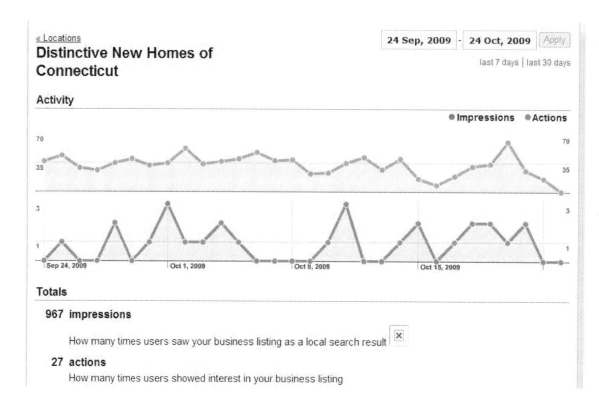

> ➢ **You can upload photos and videos to your listing so people can learn more about you immediately.**
> ➢ **Clients can post reviews that can give potential customers a comfort level to use your services.**

Chapter 4: Building the Site

Warning: this gets a little technical but you can't have a site rank well without the information contained in this chapter. I don't expect you to do it yourself, you need to take this information to your web designers and/or template website companies and have them implement it. A tip about web designers: a web "designer" is not always an SEO specialist. You will most likely need someone to implement the strategies behind the scenes.

Now that you have your brand and keyword now it's time to select a URL or web address.

Selecting a URL:

- **Best is ".com"**
- **Write down 20 best names, no numbers, no dashes**
- **You CAN have multiple websites**
- **Best practices**
    - **11 Characters or less for the URL**

- http://instantdomainsearch.com/ **this is a free service that looks up your URL's in real time as you type.**
- **Tip: if you can use your main keyword as your URL you can rank faster eg.** newhomesct**.com I used newhomesct right in the URL-- that will help my site rank more quickly.**

Building the site: "Tagging"

The language of Google and all search engines is HTML. When Google searches a site for relevant content it looks ON the page and OFF the page.

Let's look at the **OFF page** information first:

To see what is "behind" a website—I will use one of my client's sites for the example--http://thenowpass.com.

To find the tags right click your mouse on the web page and then click "view source" or "view page source"— these are their website "tags":

<title> Washington DC Bus Tours | DC Sightseeing Tours | Now Pass DC</title>

<meta name**="description" content**="The Now Pass DC offers savings up to 40% on transportation and admission to the most popular Washington, DC attractions and up to 80% on dining and other Washington, DC tours." />

<meta name**="keywords" content="**washington dc bus tour, dc sightseeing tours, double decker bus tours, washington dc tours, bus rides" />

BEST PRACTICES: Tagging

TITLE TAG   Upper left side of webpage on the browser
MOST important to Google--- no more than 70 characters.

Example

Meta description – do this for EVERY page, change the tags to match content.

Meta keyword – change the keywords or add to homepage keywords

Example of poor keyword content:

Connecticut Homes,Houses for Sale,Community info,New Haven County,School,Properties land,Homes in North Haven Durham,cheshire wallingford,Homes for sale,residential,Listings,real estate,homes for sale, homes, agent, realtor, house, residential, broker, single family, condominium, townhouse, buy,buyer commercial, development,estate,for sale by owner,fsbo,investment,listing,luxury homes,mls,multiple listing,multiple listing service,new construction,realty,relo,relocation,second homes">

Example of targeted content:

real estate Connecticut,connecticut real estate,connecticut real estate for sale,connecticut real estate listings,real estate agencies in connecticut,real estate for sale in connecticut,Connecticut homes for sale

Example of niche content: Stamford ct homes for sale, Stamford ct real estate, Stamford ct condos, Stamford area real estate

Remember to change the Title, meta and description tags for EACH PAGE. Google likes to see a website that is well put together and complete. It takes time but it will be worth it in the end.

There is a lot of talk in the search engine community about whether or not the meta data keywords are related to search position. While they are not as relevant to your page rank as in the past, the consensus is they are important enough to at least include. Don't try to keyword "stuff" and throw the kitchen sink of keywords in there. Stick to 10 or 20 relevant keyword or keyword phrases.

ON Page CONTENT—Why pretty websites finish last….

What I mean by pretty, the site beautiful on the outside but not much on the inside. A good website should have an element of design of course but the rules of SEO should not be ignored in favor of lots of flashy pictures, etc.

When you do your research and see what sites rank high on Google for your keywords, you will notice one thing in common, CONTENT. Unless you are an authority site like macys.com, or some other well-known company that has been around a long time, you will need to coax Google into realizing you're there. The way to do this is with good keyword rich content. Google "spiders" eat this up!

Content is KING --this is the best way for Google to determine relevancy—make sure your homepage has a nice 250-500 words of keyword rich content and BOLD the ranking keywords.

Check out your competition for your keywords. See what they are doing and what words they include. This will help you when you are designing your site.

Another thing to consider is that Google only reads HTML content, meaning, pictures must be tagged with words and Flash is not readable by Google spiders. Make sure your site doesn't use too much of anything that is not "spider"-friendly.

This probably goes without saying but a big thing is once you get them there, you want them to STAY. Make sure the site is easy to navigate and invites the customer to stay awhile. According to the research, people come to your website FIRST for information, not to buy.

Chapter 5: Link Building Using Online Classifieds

So, we've learned how to find the niche we want to target, how to build the site to satisfy Google spider's appetite, now what? Why aren't I number 1 already?

Besides getting your website set up properly. The best way to describe ranking is a popularity contest – how popular are you? How Google determines popularity is LINKS. This means your URL appearing on websites relevant to your site. How many people are linking to your website and even more important, how many of those sites are popular? The more popular a site is (known as an authority site) that links to you, the more weight the link gets.

Link Building 101

First start with any businesses with which you are affiliated, suppliers etc—make sure they are relevant. Approach them about putting a link on their site to yours. You can trade links with them as well, set up a resources or services page and put their links on it.

IMPORTANT: When creating backlinks always use your keywords next to the link, NEVER say "click here". "Click here" is not a keyword! Use your keywords, example: For more Washington, DC tour information http://thenowpass.com or "embed" your link behind your keywords (called an anchor text link—I have a code later on in the book for your reference)

Creating Links Using Craig's List and other Classified Sites:

Post to Craig's List, ebay classifieds, and backpage.com to create backlinks .

Some of these sites use what is called "no follow links" meaning that Google doesn't necessarily give them a lot of weight but your keyword associated with your website does so even if it's a no follow site, it is better than nothing especially when it's FREE. Don't worry about trying to "sell" your product on Craig's list, etc. post it anyway, people do check for products and services, you may get an interested person.

Example of Good Craig's list post:

GREENWICH NYC SUBURB BRAND NEW CONDO <$1M 2400SF (Manhattan) - 899,000

THANK YOU FOR LOOKING AT MY AD

FEATURED PROPERTY GREENWICH CONDO WWW.GREENWICHCONDO .COM APPROX $374 PER SF, 2 BEDROOMS AND AN OFFICE SPACE, STORAGE NOT AN OFFER WHERE PRIOR REGISTRATION REQUIRED-- DEVELOPMENT LOCATED ON RIVER IN GREENWICH CT, 1 CAR GARAGE, 1 ADD'L ASSIGNED SPACE, MARBLE TILE, GRANITE COUNTERTOPS, VIKING APPLIANCES, PANTRY OFF KITCHEN, TAXES LOW EST $6300/YR, LOW COMMON CHARGES, $350/MO

FOR MORE GREENWICH TOWNHOME INFORMATION WWW.GREENWICHCONDO.COM

Chapter 6 : Online Press Releases For Link Building

Many people miss this opportunity. In the past, press releases were sent to get your news in the newspaper or picked up on a news show some kind of traditional press. Today, we use online press release sites to announce things, yes, but also part of a link building strategy. You can send out an online press release on pretty much anything.

Here are some ideas of what to send press releases on:

- Announce your site and what it's about

- Announce that your business has joined the social networks, Facebook, Twitter, etc.

- Announce a sale or a special

- Promote a speaking engagement or an award you received

- Announce the winner of a contest or your 1000th customer

Each one of these produces a backlink to your site. I recommend at least 1 per month.

There are great free press release sites like http://www.free-press-release.com/ and others (I have provided you a list of many more in the resource section of this book). However there are paid sites that I also use that can give you more "link juice" then the free ones. I only recommend using these if you have a big announcement; prweb.com is one I like to use. I use them once every other month but a free site is just fine for most of these types of link building efforts.

Chapter 7: Creating Links through Article Writing

Article sites have HUGE authority with Google. That is because they are extremely strict about what content can be included. You cannot use any promotional language in the articles, they must be written like news articles.

One of the top article sites (I have included others in your resource section), is Ezinearticles.com

 You are allowed 10 initial article submissions, then you can qualify for platinum status and they will let you post unlimited articles.

Write articles on your blog or website's topic. You can use blog post content for articles just make sure it is not promotional in any way and is in the third person. Don't worry if someone else has written something on your subject, the point is to gain backlinks for your site.

Most article sites will not allow you to post links to your site within the article itself, you will have to use "anchor text" links to post links. Anchor text links are the text links highlighted in blue and underlined that when you click on them takes you to a web page.

To create an anchor text link, use the following format:

<a href=" http://www.YOURWEBSITE.com ">YOUR KEYWORD </a>

Chapter 8: Creating Links Through Directory Submissions

When I first began learning SEO, I had no idea that there were directories around the web for the sole purpose of keeping track of web pages--like the "yellow pages" of web pages for instance. Search engines love directories and you will be ranked higher if you are included.

Web directories are essentially lists of links which are organized by topic so people can find your site when looking on the internet for information and resources. Like the yellow pages, using a web directory, people can find lists of website on related topics which complement each other. For example, someone who is looking for parenting magazines could use a directory and find them organized by type, such as teen parenting, baby, toddler, etc.

These directories are not considered search engines in and of themselves, although you can search a directory to find the topic that you are looking for. Rather, they consist of a collection of links which are updated on a regular basis to ensure that they are relevant and useful. Many search engines have their own directories (i.e. Yahoo).

There are a number of ways in which web directories can be put together. Some, like DMOZ --one of the most powerful directories on the web, are built entirely by hand, with editors personally checking each link which is included in the directory. You can submit your listing but it will take some time and must be submitted properly.

Others are built by computers scouring the web using a variety of ways to determine which links are relevant for which topics. You can also pay for placement in some directories like Yahoo and I recommend that if you want to rank quickly, you consider that as a viable option. Yahoo has one of the oldest directories on the web.

I have included a list of web directories in the resource section of this book.

Chapter 6: Creating Links Using Blogs

A lot of people ask, do I need a blog…in a word YES! If for no other reason then you build backlinks with this. You can hire someone to write blog posts for you, but make sure these people understand your "voice" and understand your product.

Most blog sites are free, wordpress, blogger, etc. Many websites are now "wordpress" websites that come with a blog installed that you can update on a regular basis.

Wordpress blogs are a great authority blog that Google LOVES. Go and check it out www.wordpress.com Set up a blog on wordpress for your niche. Post at least once per week. Now with the new Google search algorithm, "caffeine" I recommend blogging once per DAY if you want to get on top of the search engines and stay there.

Sounds like a lot? Don't worry, I'll give you some ideas to get you going and most blog posts can be short, 250 words and with most if not all of the blog platforms, you can schedule your blog posts so when you have time write 10 or so and then schedule them. This way you have fresh content populating your website or blog at all times.

There are many reasons to start a blog but in this book I am going to focus on specifically using blogs to build backlinks to your website. Remember though, a blog is a place where people gather to converse about topics or offer information it is NOT an advertising or press release tool—you can post releases just make sure they are not too "salesy."

Do not overtly sell in the blog. BAD example "to buy my napkins click here" content is important and you can embed links to your site within your blog. To "embed" a link, highlight the text and click on the "chain-looking" icon on the toolbar.

When embedding links, it is best practice to "open in new window" so they don't have to hit the back button to go to back to your blog.

If you are using a blog site separate from your website, just be careful and make sure for every link you embed to **your** site, you have embedded 1 or 2 others to places like "Wikipedia" or any other RELATED—a non-commercial site. Because blogs are supposed to be places where people share information, blog sites will kick you out if you try and use them too overtly to SELL. By linking to other non-commercial sites, you show that you are interested in giving information, not just gaining sales. You can pay for a blog site on wordpress but why not just follow the rules and use the free one?

As I mentioned, blog posts don't need to be long, 250 words are plenty. You can even embed your YouTube videos in your blogs.

Top 20 GREAT Blog Ideas

Idea #1

Ask questions. Use your social networks, Twitter, Facebook and LinkedIn groups. Use these networks to ask questions of your friends, fans and connections. Questions like, what do you like about (enter your business or niche)? How do you choose the right (enter your product or service here)? What are your "burning" questions about (enter your product or service here).

When folks answer these questions, you can get great blog topics. Take their answers and use them as a blog post, then add some of your own content. It's a great way to get the conversation started.

Idea #2

Blog about what your **clients ALWAYS ask you**. You know your business better than anyone and I'm sure you have a list of questions you get asked all the time. Write down the top 10 and do one blog post every day answering those questions.

Folks always say, "someone else has written that already." Who cares? If that was true then your clients wouldn't ask, would they? You can use these not only for blog posts but for email subject lines to get your clients engaged. And, don't forget if you are on Twitter, Facebook and Linkedin you can pull your blog posts into your profiles and pages so you can TRIPLE your exposure.

Idea #3

LISTS. People LOVE lists! Look at any grocery store magazine rack and you will see the same information over and over again in lists just said a little differently. "Top 10 ways to lose weight," etc. What about top 5 things you should look for in a (enter your profession here)? Top 10 reasons why you need to become an entrepreneur, etc.

Idea #4

Sales reports. Come up with sales statistics for your product and talk about the market. Using already generated reports is okay, only change things around to make them your own. NOTE: **DO NOT copy someone else's content without their permission**. If you do, be sure to credit them and give a link back to their post.

Idea #5

Give something away. Create a "free report" or ebook to give away and build your list at the same time. Remember when I said to ask questions and use lists? Take this information and re-purpose it into a "free" report on items related to your field. Start off the blog post and then ask them to download your free report but they have to sign up for your email list.

Idea #6

Interview industry experts. Interview a client or service provider that complements your business or service and ask them questions. Examples could be a local business owner, marketer or successful sales person. Post the Q&A as is on your blog.

Idea #7

Interview local celebrities, politicians. Maybe there is a local spin you can use to promote your product or business or perhaps there is someone in your community that is a local hero or well known author or celebrity in your area. Ask them for an interview.

Idea #8

Reviews. Review products, people, things related to your service or product or any other kind of review you can think of. Always keep it positive. Also, these can become viral—alert the person that they have been reviewed and they will likely forward it to friends, post it on their Facebook or other social networks.

Idea #9

Link Fest --Write a post that includes a list of links to other blog posts or pages that publish great content. You can write about an article you saw relating to your industry as long as you credit the original author.

Idea #10

Solve problems. Let them know what to be afraid of and then be their solution. Example, top 5 things that can stop your business from growing; how YOU are preventing your product from selling; how you can prevent client horror stories; how to protect your reputation from a poor customer service experience, bad product, and the like.

Idea #11

Write a "How to." These are really popular because selling a product/service is not only a financial investment, it is so

VERY personal. Prove your expertise by helping them navigate the waters.

Don't worry if you've covered some of these topics in your other posts, again, remember the magazine example? Cosmo and Oprah magazines re-use the same content ALL the time, they just say it differently. And as long as you at least write a new introduction, it won't hurt your SEO strategy.

Idea #12

Truth telling. Do a fact or fiction blog. Example Fiction: I can't benefit from your product in this economy Fact: Yes you can and explain how.

Fiction: I can't afford it right now. Fact: Here are the top things that will add value and tell them what they are.

Idea #13

Tell them some **insider information**. People love to be on the inside. Example: Showcase news bites, reviews and testimonials or announce upcoming products or promotions of your business.

Idea #14

Talk about your products. Now, as a general rule blogs are NOT PLACES TO SELL THINGS. You can do a "review" of your product and just give the facts and a link to your website or youtube video. Don't put prices or announce sales or anything like that. If you are using a generic blog site, they will block you if you try and sell things constantly.

Idea #15

Do a feature on your community. You live and work in your community and you want to establish yourself as THE go-to expert for your community. Why wouldn't they want to purchase from you if you are a well recognized expert? Do very easy stuff, like demographics, history, architecture and then talk about product info. Don't forget to ask them to sign up for your newsletter to get more information.

Idea #16

Share some personal stories. It has been said that people do business with people they like, know and trust. Establishing that trust is as much personal as it is business and most likely, YOU are YOUR BRAND so you want potential clients to get to know you. Recipes, funny personal anecdotes and sharing the list of books you are reading are a great way for people to get to know you.

Idea #18

Be the event source. Blog about the local events that are happening in your community or national events happening in your industry. Do a community calendar or review great events that you attended from around your market area.

Idea #19

Comparisons. People love comparisons. Compare product appreciation over time (most likely over time, products or services will pay for themselves). Compare products (again keep it positive), compare competition (use independent data), compare ANYTHING in your field that will keep readers coming back for more.

Idea #20

Do a video blog post. Video is a great way to build credibility. Use a flip cam and don't just talk about how to use your product, SHOW THEM. Show everything from opening the box to using it in real world applications. Give them another way to interact with you. You can use all of the social networking platforms to pull your videos in, Facebook, Twitter and Linkedin.

Bonus Idea: Offer complementary business partners the opportunity to write content FOR you. They can be guest bloggers for you. Offer them the opportunity to write about their expertise, credit them and give them a link back to their website. It's a great way to build relationships with potential joint venture partners and get new content for your site.

Chapter 6: Social Bookmarking

You may have seen these icons hanging around the web and wondered what they were?

Social Bookmarking is an integral part of a well-developed link building strategy. I will start by covering what social bookmarking is.

According to Wikipedia.org; "Social Bookmarking is a method for Internet users to share, organize, search, and manage bookmarks of web resources. Unlike file sharing, the resources themselves aren't shared, merely bookmarks that reference them."

Here is my "social bookmarking for dummies like me" definition:

There are over 13 billion webpages on the internet. To organize all of our favorite content, we need ways to pick out the best pages and save them for later. You have choices, you can bookmark or add to favorites in our web browser but that can become a huge list (my husband used to laugh at me because I probably had 500 pages "bookmarked"), plus, these bookmarks are only associated with one computer. If you sign in on another computer at work or while you're away on vacation, you won't be able to see your bookmarks. This is how "social" bookmarking got its start.

In addition, this way you can share your bookmarks with others who may want to read the article or blog post you just saved. Think of it as clipping a newspaper article and copying it and passing it around to others. It is the same principle.

For instance, you are a local food blogger and socially bookmark your favorite restaurants and wine stores. Someone who is interested in dining in your area could come across your bookmarked pages and read them. Another example, you are a realtor who used bookmarking to save relevant real estate related articles or you bookmark your listings. You organize things but it is public instead of private on your personal computer.

You may wonder why you would want everyone to see what websites you visit, but as a marketer this is not such a bad thing. Bookmarks are not only public and visible to other surfers; they are also visible to the search engines and are indexed quite frequently by them . Put simply a website that may have taken weeks to be indexed by the search engines can now be indexed in a matter of days.

You want people to bookmark YOUR site to help you build backlinks. There are paid services that bookmark your content but better to have it happen naturally and have clients and other influencers bookmark your site.

Benefits of Bookmarking:

- It helps you build a great deal of backlinks.
- It helps increase your traffic.
- Your link gets indexed by Google in a matter of minutes.
- It's free!

These links combined with other advanced Link Building tactics such as: (Directory Submission, Press Syndication, Forum Signatures, Blog Commenting, etc…) should form a formidable linking strategy.

I have also found that bookmarks have a way of showing up on the first page of the search engines for some long tail keywords, weeks before my home page showed up for my desired keyword. Bookmarks are there, kind of like holding the position.

Now that we covered what social bookmarking is, let's find out how you can use it to your advantage. For social bookmarking to be effective, the golden rules of internet marketing apply. These rules are time tested and should all be used as a basis for all link building campaigns. Make sure you create good content that people WANT to bookmark. Don't Sell! No-one wants to be sold, especially not in a social setting. You don't want to be labeled as a spammer!

Here is an example of a Social Bookmark Site:

URL is the location of the content you are bookmarking. In most case this is a deep page on your website

Example: http://yourwebsie/your-longtail-keyword

Titles are important because this is the first thing the search engine sees and just like the meta tags on your website this is an important ranking factor for your social bookmarks.

Example: (Long Tail Keyword) New Dog Training Ideas

Body (description): Descriptions are added to bookmarks in the form of metadata, so that other users may understand the content of the resource without first needing to download it for themselves, As usual in social media you should avoid trying to sell to the intended target and inform them instead.

Example: Cool article that explains (your keyword)

Keep it to 75 to 250 characters depending on the social bookmarking website.

Social tagging is used to classify the content of your bookmark

Example: social media training, internet marketing, social media, training, business

Note: A great semi-automatic Social Bookmarking Service is www.socialmarker.com, this free tool allows **Semi-Automated Submission** to 50+ social bookmarking sites! It can help you spread a link on 50 of the best social bookmarking sites in fewer than 15 minutes!

Top social bookmarking websites:

- del.icio.us: It allows you to easily add sites you like to your personal collection of links and to categorize those sites with keywords. Not to mention that if enough people save your site in a bookmark, it will make their popular page list and send a lot of traffic. Delicious is owned by Yahoo and is a MUST for your social media and bookmarking strategy.
- StumbleUpon: Owned by eBay, StumbleUpon is an amazing blend of social bookmarking, voting, networking, web surfing, search and blogging. Best of all, StumbleUpon can send major traffic with its userbase of around 3 million users.
- Digg: The social news site that changed the Internet, Digg is a high power authority and a listing in Digg for a site, even if it only has a couple of votes, will rank highly on Google and other search engines for certain terms. If your site is shared and voted upon on Digg, and makes the Digg homepage, you'll get a lot of traffic and attention from other bloggers who read Digg.

- Furl: Furl.net is widely considered one of the first social bookmarking sites and is an authority by the major search engines. Listing your sites in Furl will lead to traffic from organic rankings and its popular page drives traffic.
- Google: Allows users to save and create bookmarks in their Google toolbar that can be accessed anywhere online.
- Reddit: Timely and shocking news oriented, Reddit stories are instantly voted upon and if liked by the community as a whole, can drive incredible traffic and users.
- Searchles : Owned by the DumbFind search engine, In my opinion, Searchles is a much overlooked bookmarking tool and loved by Google, Yahoo and the other major search engines with its passing of link juice and high rankings for terms within search results themselves.
- Yahoo! Bookmarks: This is the MOST POPULAR social bookmarking service on the internet. A great

feature of Yahoo Bookmarks is that they let users store bookmarks using their Yahoo Toolbar and access them from any computer.

Chapter 7: Analyzing Your Site

Great news! There is another free tool: Google Analytics
http://www.Google.com/analytics/

Installing analytics to your site is as simple as installing a tracking code.

Fill out your website URL and the account name. If you are monitoring several websites make sure you name the site so you can recognize it quickly.

Once you sign up you get your tracking code:

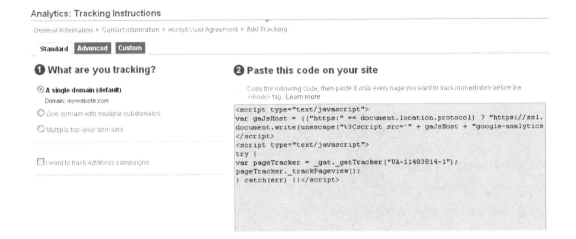

Analytics: Tracking Instructions

General Information > Contact Information > Accept User Agreement > Add Tracking

Standard **Advanced** **Custom**

1 What are you tracking?

A single domain (default)
Domain: mywebsite.com

One domain with multiple subdomains

Multiple top-level domains

I want to track AdWords campaigns

2 Paste this code on your site

Copy the following code, then paste it onto every page you want to track immediately before the \<body\> tag. Learn more

```
<script type="text/javascript">
var gaJsHost = (("https:" == document.location.protocol) ? "https://ssl.
document.write(unescape("%3Cscript src='" + gaJsHost + "google-analytics
</script>
<script type="text/javascript">
try {
var pageTracker = _gat._getTracker("UA-11483814-1");
pageTracker._trackPageview();
} catch(err) {}</script>
```

There are instructions on there as to how to get the code to place in your website. Many SEO specialists and web masters will tell you to create a different code for every page. They would be correct. However, if you're just getting started let's go in stages. The very first stage is getting the code on your homepage. If you know how to do it, go ahead and insert it but if not, make sure your web designer does it. It takes 24 hrs to get recognized and the results are 24hrs behind but for a free tool, you really can't beat it.

When you get the results, what are you looking for? NOT HITS. Hits mean NOTHING. What you want are unique visitors and look at the "bounce rate" and time on site.

Google analytics can be embedded in your site to give you information such as:

> **Number of visitors**
> **Where they are linking from?**
> **How many pages and what pages they are looking at**
> **What geographic areas are they in?**
> **What keywords they are using to find you?**

What does Bounce Rate mean?

Bounce rate is the percentage of single-page visits or visits in which the person left your site from the entrance (landing) page. Use this metric to measure visit quality - a high bounce rate generally indicates that site entrance pages aren't relevant to your visitors. The more compelling your landing pages, the more visitors will stay on your site and convert. You want a low bounce rate. For sales oriented internet marketing sites, under 70% is pretty good but for most professional websites, you want a bounce rate under 40%.

Many template sites offer their own brand of analytics, you should make sure they also include Google analytics, besides being free, it is one of the most comprehensive analytic tools out there.

Analytics Goals

Google even allows you to set goals for your website. This way you can measure your success against the amount of traffic you would like to get to your site.

Video Chapter 1: Video Marketing

Why Video?

Online video is one of the best social media tools to engage an audience and build a great deal of authority backlinks for your site.

With online video you can also reach a huge audience for a minimal investment, thus the **ROI of online video marketing** can be astounding.

- ➢ **52% of all web traffic is video (according to industry watchdog, *eMarketer*)**
- ➢ **More than 70% of all web visitors watch online video (according *to New York Times*)**
- ➢ **The average YouTube visitor spends 27 minutes watching video per day**
- ➢ **The search engines visit video sites every few minutes so your videos appear in Google, Yahoo and MSN just MINUTES after you submit, not days or weeks**

- Because video is so popular, video links and clips often show up before other content
- 77% of users coming to YouTube come intending to watch only 1 video but end up watching several.

As you can see by the statistics, video marketing can be extremely powerful tools in the attempts to engage with your market and rank your website. One of the most frequently asked questions when first starting with video marketing is: "Do I need a professional video made in order to promote my products and services online?" The answer is "no." Go out to YouTube right now and search for what would be relevant to your profession, market or industry. What do the videos that have been viewed the most have in common? You can bet it's not for their professional quality; it's about **information.** Does the video provide the person watching with the information they need? If the answer is "Yes", then those are the ones that get the most views.

How long does your video need to be? According to SmartMarket media, and TubeMogul:

Most videos steadily lose viewers once "play" is clicked, with an average 10.39% of viewers clicking away after ten seconds and 53.56% leaving after one minute.

What does that mean for you and your business? Video is not the place to be long-winded. Answer the question and provide the information quickly. Another take-away from this is that if you are going to ask someone to buy your product or service, start the video with making your sales pitch. Don't make it long; just make sure it's there in the first 10 seconds. You can use a voice-over or use an overlay or an "annotation."   Annotations will be covered later in this guidebook.

Video Chapter 2: Getting Started on YouTube

There are many great video sites out there and when making your decision on where to start, pick the one with the highest rankings and most widely used by the majority of online communities. YouTube is a large authority in and of itself and, of course, it always helps when you're owned by Google, like they are. Facebook and Google are fighting for the number one search engine spot but YouTube is still the number 2 or 3 depending upon the week. For purposes of this guidebook, I will focus the number one video sharing site, YouTube.

It is really very simple to get started with YouTube. I recommend setting up a free Gmail address, that's a Google email account. Google owns YouTube so they make it easier to sign up with a Gmail account. Also, this way you can set up YouTube easily and keep all of your video emails out of your normal email inbox. You can set up a YouTube account without a Gmail account, but I find it easier and faster with a Gmail account set up.

To get started on YouTube, go to http://youtube.com and click "create account."

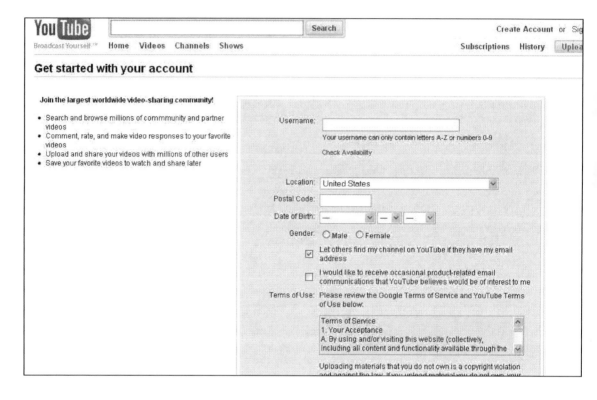

You will be asked for your date of birth. This is because of privacy standards which require that users be at least 13 years old in order to have a YouTube account.

Your user name will turn into your "channel" name so put some thought into this. If you represent your brand, make the channel name your own. A wise move would be to name it by using a keyword that is relevant to your business.

In any case, you want the channel to represent not only YOU and YOUR BUSINESS, you also want to make it easy for online searchers to FIND you and your business channel on YouTube. Once you have filled out all of the information and clicked on create account you will come to this screen:

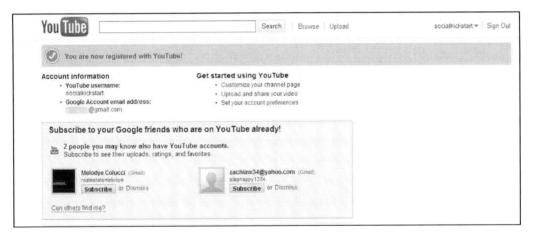

I recommend that you set up your account properly before sharing information and videos with the rest of the world. When you click on account preferences you will get this screen:

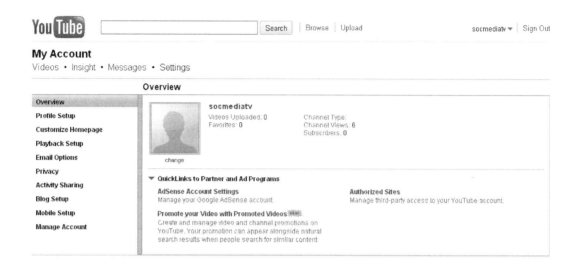

(if you already have a YouTube account go to the upper right where it has your account/channel name, click on the drop down box and click "account")

Click on Profile setup and you will get here:

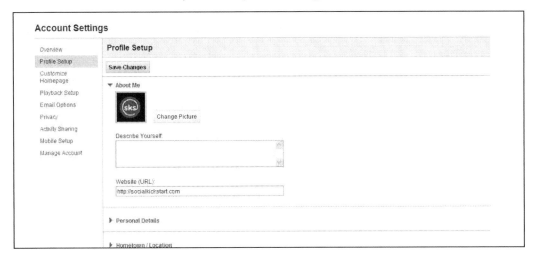

It is important, like with all the social networks, that you set up your profile to accurately reflect yourself and/or your organization. Either upload a good picture of yourself here or a logo for your company, whichever is a better fit for your primary purpose in using YouTube.

Fill out as much relevant information as you feel comfortable sharing and click "save changes."

The next area is "customize homepage". Here you are not actually "customizing" the design of the home page, just which modules you and your viewers will see on the channel's homepage. There are many different modules as you can see. Best to leave the default until you are engaging on the network and you can change these at any time.

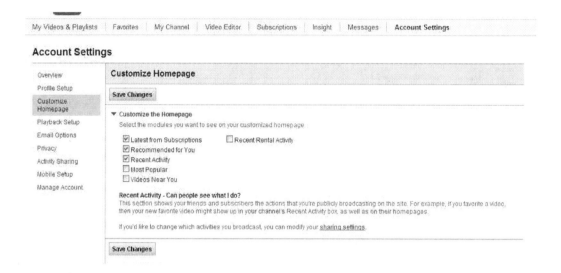

Next in this area is "playback setup." In this area you decide how you want the videos to play back on your computer. If you have a dial up modem or a slow connection you may want to adjust this.

You can also click on "captions" and "annotations" and decide if you want to view these or not. I like to leave them in tact but it is entirely your choice.

In the "Email Options" screen you let Youtube know what language and how often you would like emails sent to you.

Privacy settings:

In the privacy settings area you can decide how you want people to share your videos and find you on YouTube.

You can also decide if you want to be targeted for ads on Youtube and whether or not the statistics and data on your video are shared with your viewers. These are completely your discretion.

Activity Sharing:

In this area you decide if and what you would like to share about your activities on YouTube. Again, this is totally up to you and I recommend you check these and decide the best choices for you.

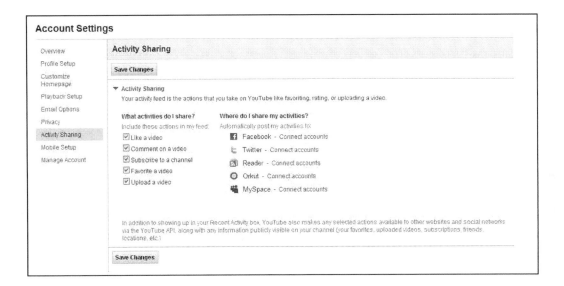

Mobile Set-up

In this area, you will get an email address that will allow you to upload videos directly to your channel from your mobile device. Some phones have a YouTube application or another way to upload them but if you do not have a smart phone, you can use this custom email address to upload your videos.

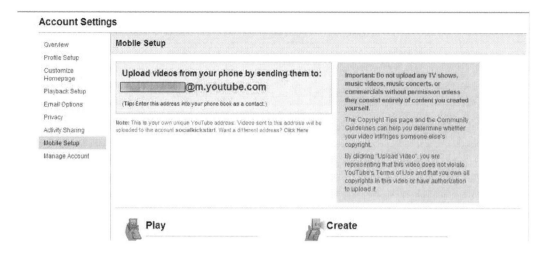

Manage Account

In this section you can change your password, delete your account or learn if your account is in violation of community guidelines or copyright infringement. If you are having issues uploading videos, I would come here to check if there are any issues that may be preventing it.

Video Chapter 3: Customizing your channel

At this point you are ready to customize your channel, pick the type of channel and make the colors and design your own.

To access the custom settings area, go to the upper right hand corner, click on the drop down and select "my channel" or click on the navigation bar "my channel".

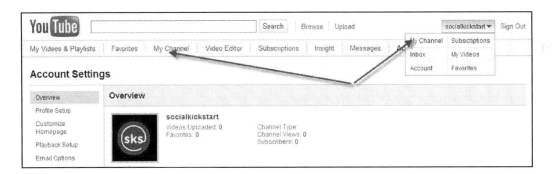

You will see this screen:

Youtube has started allowing channel managers to post "bulletins", like status updates from Facebook onto their pages and send to their channel subscribers. At this point you most likely won't have any subscribers so you can skip it but you may want to post "Glad to be here on YouTube" or some kind of a welcome message.

Start with 3 steps

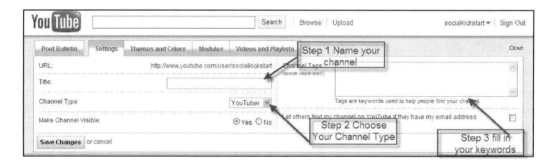

First start with the "settings" area on the navigation tabs. The first thing you want to do is give your channel a name. It could be the name of your company or a keyword that is relevant to your business.

Step 2 --One thing that most people don't know is that there are different types of accounts you can choose to represent you best on YouTube: Youtuber, Director, Musician, Comedian, Guru and Reporter.

Here is the YouTube help explanation of the different channel types:

All accounts share the basic features on YouTube like uploading, commenting, sharing, video responses, etc. Each of the specialized account types offers different customization options:

Director:

Allows customized "Performer Info" to be displayed on your Profile page, describing yourself, your influences and your style.

Musician:

Allows custom logo, genre and tour date information, and CD purchase links on your Profile page.

Comedian:

Allows custom logo, style and show date information, and CD purchase links on your Profile page.

Guru:

Allows custom logo, genre and links on your Profile page.

Reporter:

Allows you to describe your Beat, your Influences, and your Favorite News Sources.

If none of these channel types fit you or your business, leaving it "Youtuber" is fine.

Then, go to the right and type in tags that reflect your video content, such as "social media training", "learn facebook", etc. use tags from your keyword list. This is how people find you on YouTube, from your tags and keywords.

Again, like your presence on all of the social networks, your YouTube presence should be branded to you and/or your company.

Branding your YouTube channel:

To brand your YouTube channel follow these simple steps:

Go up on the next tab "Themes and Colors"

From here you can change the themes, change the colors and also move around the "modules" on your channel page.

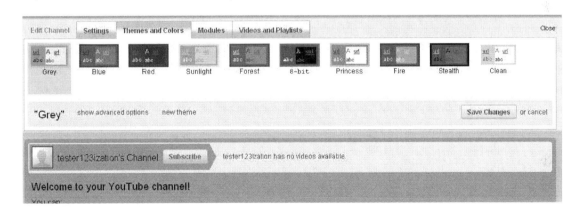

You can use one of their color schemes if they best represent you and your business or you can upload your own background image and change fonts and colors.

To further enhance and customize the look of your channel page click on "Show Advanced Options". Then you will come to this screen:

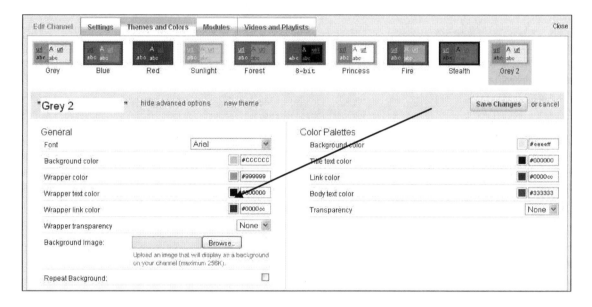

Much like Facebook fan pages or Twitter backgrounds, YouTube also allows you to upload a custom channel design. Keep in mind some design tips:

Page Dimensions: The content area that contains your videos and profile information is 960 pixels wide. You will be creating a layout to "surround" that area. Your background image will be displayed below the white

YouTube bar at the top, so you should begin your content at the very top of your image, and on either side of the 960 pixel center column. A good total image size, which should account for most monitor resolutions, is 2000 x 2200 pixels.

Maximum File Size: 256 KB (preferably JPEG format)

Layout: Your image will automatically be centered on your channel page. This means that important image content (like logos or graphic elements that "frame" your profile) should appear just to the left and right of the 960 pixel center column without going behind it.

To upload your background image, go to background image on the bottom left, click browse and upload a custom background or your logo. There are companies that create custom YouTube channel backgrounds very inexpensively. If YouTube is going to be one of the main social networks you use, I highly recommend hiring someone to customize all of your social network properties so the branding is consistent.

Modules Area

This is where you can customize which modules you would like shown on the homepage of your channel. You can see the choices below and in the next screen shot you see how they correspond to the areas on your channel below:

I recommend that you leave all options checked because comments, recent activity, and friends are all important if you want to build a community around your YouTube channel.

You can also click on "edit" next to each of the modules and customize each module if you would like. You can also use the down and up arrows to move the channel modules around to further customize your channel.

Video and Playlist:

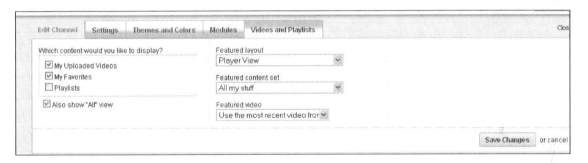

In here be sure you select "Use the most recent video" in the "Featured video" area, that way people will view your latest video as soon as they land on your channel. Also make sure you keep the featured video layout to "Player

View" this will make sure people coming to your channel will see your most recent uploads.

Video Chapter 4: What do I do a video ON?

Ok now you are ready to begin uploading videos. But wait you say, I don't have a video and I don't know what to do a video on! This is something I hear all the time when I am doing seminars on video, blogging or article writing. What kind of content/videos can I create that people will read/watch? Well, let us just say that the goal here IS to connect with people in your audience and build a community. However, YouTube offers extremely valuable "back" links to your site to assist you with your search engine optimization strategy. It is advisable that you be on YouTube for this reason alone.

Let's talk about video content:

"How To" videos are a HUGE thing on YouTube. How to's of every kind are available. Go to YouTube and see what your competitors are doing. Just because a video has been done doesn't mean you can't create one too. Search engines love new content, therefore your video could possibly outrank the one that is already there, simply by being new. It is extremely important to note here that YOU DO NOT COPY someone else's content. Use your own and put your own spin on it.

Answer questions. Ask your audience, customers, etc. what their most "burning" questions are about what you do. Or just reach back and make a list of the top questions you get all the time. Answer one question per day in your video post.

Make a funny video. How-to's and funny videos get the most play on YouTube. Try and think of a funny topic and do the video based on that. Remember, however, if you are using this for your business, you want to make sure the joke is not on you.

Lists—people LOVE lists. "The Top 10 Ways To Promote Your Business Online", "The Top 10 Things You Can Do To Lose Weight ", etc. Challenge yourself to start right away by making one video per day for the next 10 days. This will help you with the start of creating your video library and populating your channel.

The videos don't have to be long. I mentioned that according to the research:

Most videos steadily lose viewers once "play" is clicked, with an average 10.39% of viewers clicking away after ten seconds and 53.56% leaving after one minute.

Keep your videos short and to the point but make sure you always offer **good content**. Nothing annoys people more than watching a how-to video that doesn't tell them "how-to."

Let's see how some of the big brands use YouTube to create a community. By studying some of these case studies, you can glean many important tips and strategies that you can apply in your own business. Videos quickly go viral online if they are entertaining, funny, and even surprising.

Although all the themes of these case studies are different, they seem to use three psychological patterns to win over the viewer:

1. **They raise the mood level.**

   They start with either a depressed person or an emotionally-neutral person and end with a crescendo of high emotion. The viewer feels their own mood level rise and they tend to think of the highlighted product much more favorably.

2. **They are larger than life.**

   Another psychological pattern used is being crazy, hilarious, and outrageous. It's about shock value and thinking outside the box. People do in videos what you would never see them do in real life. This adds a pleasant shock value that makes viewers inclined to post them on links on social media like Facebook or Twitter. Often music and special effects are blended in to create an "aha" experience for the viewer.

3. They use music to change mood levels. Finally, music often plays a role in winning the viewer over, and it has the same effect as does music played in the background of a movie. It works to change the mood and make the viewer more receptive to the marketing message.

Here are a couple of case studies I found that use some of the tactics highlighted above:

The Weezer Case Study: Weezer, an alternative rock band, created a video called "Pork and Beans," to promote their group. They gathered a collection of Youtube Internet superstars to create something both amusing and delightful. Their marketing approach is fresh and innovative:

In short order, they assembled the following cast of well know YouTube "celebrities":

• Tay Zonday, famous for Chocolate Rain.

• The notorious Blendtec blender from "Will it Blend?"

• The gorgeous Miss Teen South Carolina.

• The Romanian Numa Numa video.

• Peanut Butter Jelly Time.

• The Ninja fool.

• The man who broke the Guinness Book of World Records for donning the most T shirts.

In essence, what the group did was to collect all the videos that were already working, select the best scenes, and put them together in a crazy, high-energy blend. These memes—a cultural idea or symbol-- were already entrenched in the social consciousness of YouTube addicts. They just brought them out to somehow reflect on their own unique brand.

Here are the statistics on how well this campaign did. Since May 23rd, 2010, it has been viewed by well over 4 million viewers.

Tips:

- Be creative, even crazily creative.

- Identify your target market.

- Find out what they already like.

- Bring it all together and tie it in with your brand or product.

The Blendtec Case Study--George Wright, Blendtec's Vice President of Marketing and Sales, understands the shock value of videos.

Blendtec, a division of K-TEC, is a blender with a powerful motor and durable materials used for commercial use. The Utah manufacturer sells their blenders to restaurants that blend drinks like smoothies, milkshakes, cappuccinos, and frozen drinks all day long.

Recognizing the huge online audience who enjoyed videos, Wright has created a whole series of videos for YouTube. The series uses a provocative question for quick identification. It is called "Will It Blend?"

In the videos, the company founder, Tom Dickson, is dressed up as a lab technician, complete with a white coat, safety glasses, and construction gloves. This immediately sets the stage for the viewer to unconsciously think of "industrial strength" appliances.

Dickson begins the videos by asking: "Will it blend? That is the question." He implies that he doesn't know and that he and the viewer are about to conduct a crazy science experiment together.

The shock value comes from his blending of expensive gadgets that nobody would even dare think of destroying.

Here are the statistics on how well this campaign has done. It has garnered 96 million views.

Tips:
- Do something outside the box.
- Create expectation by using a title that grabs attention.
- Use a spoken tag line to hook the reader.

• Wear the clothes and use the props that frame the expectations.

• Involve the reader in a discovery process, a collaborative venture.

• Do something outrageous in a straight-faced manner.

How do I make a video?

In my very first advertising class, the professor got up and said – "Whatever you do, don't star in your own commercials." Well a lot has changed since then. People want to see you and representatives of your company, they want to hear from you and know that you are authentic. Obviously, it depends upon your goals for video marketing. Are you branding yourself, your product, both? Or are you just using YouTube for the valuable back links it offers?

Depending upon your reason for using the network will dictate your level of video quality. Many videos that go "viral" are homemade and are made with nothing more than a flip cam or a cell phone video camera. Don't worry about the quality, you do not need to have fancy video and editing equipment to make a good video.

I use a **Flip** camera for the reason of simple "point – shoot - upload", and "no instructions needed" ease of use. The price is another very attractive factor with this easy camcorder: for under $200 you can make a video in HD.

Another good camera for this is the Kodak Zi8 which is good because you can add an inexpensive microphone to this like the Sony ECM-DS30p and you'll get great sound even when interviewing people or recording at conferences. There are even resources to make videos from your powerpoint slides or still photos -- I really enjoy one called Animoto, another similar service is One True Media.

I recommend you make 5-10 videos and get them in "the queue" before getting started on YouTube. Just like content is king, consistency is the hallmark of creating a community on any of the social networking sites, and the same holds true for YouTube.

Video Chapter 5: Uploading Video to YouTube

Now that your settings are taken care of and your channel is all set and you have your first video, now it's time to get started uploading videos to the channel. It's very easy to do simply click on the Upload area next to the YouTube search bar:

You will see this screen:

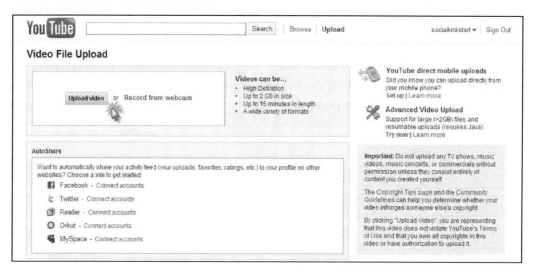

Here you can also connect all of your social networks.

Uploading tips:

Make sure they're in one of these **YouTube formats**.

Video	
Resolution	**Recommended: Original resolution of your video - for HD it is 1920x1080 (1080p) or 1280 x 720.**
Bit rate	Because bit-rate is highly dependent on codec there is no recommended or minimum value. Videos should be optimized for resolution, aspect ratio and frame rate rather than bit rate.
Frame rate	The frame rate of the original video should be maintained without re-sampling. In particular pulldown and other frame rate re-sampling techniques are strongly discouraged.
Codec	H.264 or MPEG-2 preferred.
Preferred containers	FLV, MPEG-2, and MPEG-4
Audio	
Codec	MP3 or AAC preferred
Preferred containers	FLV, MPEG-2, and MPEG-4
Sampling rate	44.1kHz
Channels	2 (stereo)

Make sure they are **not too big**. Many HD videos can be massive in size. Not only is there a limit to what YouTube will accept, it sometimes can take hours, even DAYS to upload large video files. Keep it simple and short and you can avoid this problem.

Make sure you **do not upload** content that is **not yours**. YouTube has very sophisticated technology that finds audio and video tracks that are protected by international copyright laws. Your video will be rejected before it goes live if they find copyright infringement. Your channel will be shut down if you get complaints about your material.

Click on "Upload video." Find the video you want to upload. I recommend keeping all of your video content in the "my videos" folder or another folder that will make it easier to find them. Also, because video files can be very large, you may want to consider storing them on an external hard drive or make sure you clean them off of your computer at regular intervals or your disk space will be eaten up quickly.

Once you select the video and click on it to begin the upload, you will see this screen:

This is THE most important step for maximum visibility for your website and your videos!

For **MAXIMUM RESULTS** make sure you follow these steps:

TITLE: Keyword rich title –use keywords that best describe how you think people will search to find your company or your videos -- totaling 64 or fewer characters.

Examples :

Social Media Marketing | Social Media Training

OR

Top Ten Ways to Lose Weight, Tip #1

DESCRIPTION: http://www.yourdomain.com Include short, descriptive, keyword-loaded copy that begins with your domain and includes a call to action or offer that a user will read and make them want to visit your web site. Two hundred (200) characters or less is the ideal length

Example: http://socialkickstart.com Learn how to protect your privacy on Facebook. Learn step by step, SEO, video marketing and other social networking training. Social Media training, social media marketing, learn facebook

You can switch up the URL between different pages on your website, your social networks, etc. wherever you want the traffic to go.

TAGS: Type up to 6 keyword phrases that are keywords or keyword phrases someone may use to search for your product or service. Make sure at least a couple of them are relevant to what your video is about, separated by commas. YouTube will take the commas out—that's ok.

Example: Facebook privacy training, learn social media, learn facebook

The next areas are category, privacy and sharing.

Select the most appropriate category for your video. When people are on YouTube "related" videos will come up when they are watching other channels, if your video is categorized and tagged properly, you have a better chance of coming up as a related video which will help your video get more exposure.

The sharing options are also important, here you will have a link URL directly to your video on youtube. The embed area will allow you to copy and paste the code into your website or blog and your video now will be present there as well.

Video Chapter 6: Editing Your Videos

Once your video is uploaded into your YouTube channel, click on the "Edit" button under the video:

Info and Settings

The Info and Settings tab will allow you to edit the video, the description, name and thumbnail (what shows up as the "icon" for your video).

*Note: if you change the thumbnail, it may take up to 24hrs for the change to be recognized.

Audio Swap

Let's say you don't like the music you have chosen, or the music is copyright protected. YouTube allows you to 'swap' out the audio on the track.

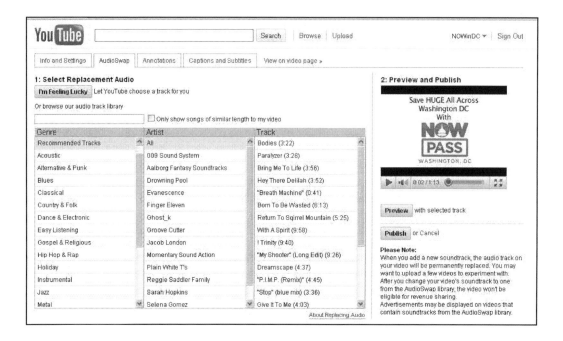

You can pick a track or have one chosen for you. You can also add music to a video that was not there before.

Annotations

Annotations are "call outs" that emphasize your call to action:

You can even place a link in the annotation box, however, YouTube does not allow you to link to a site outside of YouTube. You can put a link to another video if you like. For example, if you're doing the top 10 list idea, you can put an annotation linking them to the next video in the list or the previous video. Just a way to keep you and your clients engaged.

Captions and Subtitles

This allows you to place captions and subtitles for hearing impaired or for alternate language speakers

Video Chapter 7: Promoting Your Videos

There are many different ways to promote or share your videos.

When you are uploading your videos you can select connected accounts and the videos will automatically post to your Facebook, Twitter and Google reader

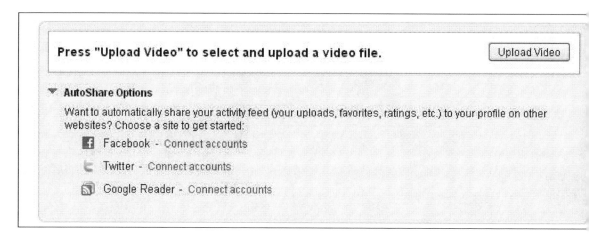

accounts.

You can also go to the main Account Settings (go up under your channel name and select "account" and set the sharing options there):

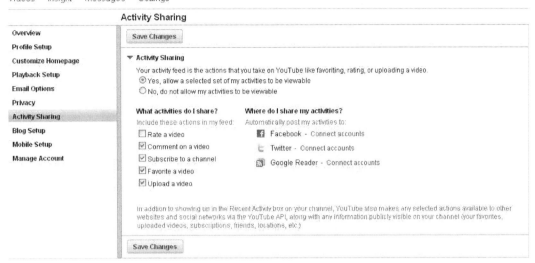

Before you check these off, make sure you keep in mind your audience and who you are connecting with on each social network. For example, if you share your professional videos on Facebook, but only have friends and family connections on Facebook, it might not be where you want the videos to be promoted.

Promote your videos on Facebook

There are 2 ways you can post videos on Facebook onto your Facebook personal profile:

LINK

Attach a link to the video that is being hosted on YouTube.

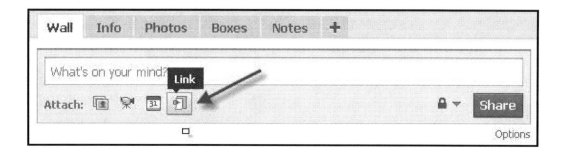

UPLOAD

Select the Wall tab and click on the Video icon.

Follow directions on the screen.

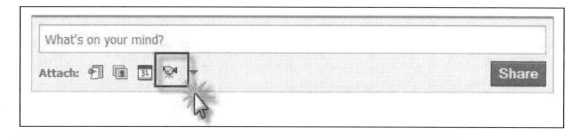

Remember that you are uploading videos to a website and if the file is too large it will take forever to upload. One of my clients sent me a 56meg video file to upload to Facebook. I queued it up and it said 22hours to upload. Not the most efficient way to upload videos.

When you are done uploading the video, click "Post" to create a description and store your video in My Videos library.

In October of 2010 Facebook removed the ability to add "applications" to your personal page. You can only add video applications to your Fan or business page.

Here are a couple of popular video applications for Facebook.

YouTube APPLICATION for Facebook

One of the most popular video applications for sharing

 videos on Facebook is YouTube Video Box. By pulling this application into your Facebook profile, or your page, you can share all your favorite YouTube videos with your friends and fans.

This application enables you to show off your favorite videos by importing them from an existing YouTube account.

To add this application to your Facebook profile, and your page, just click on the image and follow super simple instructions on the screen.

 **YouTube Channel Application**

This application allows you to synchronize your YouTube channel on your Facebook business page.

Promote your videos on Twitter

Twitter makes it super easy to share your videos with your Twitter community through services like TwitVid.com. If you have a Twitter account then you already have a TwitVid account as well.

Using TwitVid:

You can upload your videos through the site, or by using your phone. Your TwitVids can be automatically posted

and shared on YouTube, Facebook, and MySpace as soon as they are finished uploading to your TwitVid account. You can also get your TwitVid Widget and show your latest TwitVids on your website or your blog.

Things to keep in mind:

Tag your pictures and your videos with appropriate keywords.

Respect Copyright Laws and share only pictures and videos that you have the rights to, or written permission from the original owner.

Add a Video to your Linkedin Profile with Google presentations application

LinkedIn is a great resource for promoting yourself, your products and events and services. A great enhancement to your LinkedIn profile is to add video. Why video? People LOVE videos, they give a sense of who and what you are. Adding video to your profile is easy and can differentiate yourself and your profile by adding some applications, including video. There are a couple of different applications that allow you to add video, Slideshare and Google Presentation. Here I am going to go over the Google Presentation app. I found it to be easier to use than the Slideshare app, although Slideshare allows you to place 3 different videos on your profile in thumbnails, whereas the Google presentation app only allows you to show one presentation at a time. The Slideshare app also allows you to have the video play immediately upon landing on your profile—the Google Presentation does not. Both applications require you to upload your videos to YouTube prior to loading.

As I mentioned, you must have your video loaded to YouTube prior, and in order to use the Google Presentation application you will need to set up a Gmail account, but it's easy and free.

Here are the step by step instructions to add video to your LinkedIn profile:

1. Login to LinkedIn

2. Go to the top right where it says "more"

3. Go to the my applications or browse applications area

4. Add the Google Presentations application—make sure you check the boxes next to "Display on my profile", "Display on my home page", click "add application"

5. Click the "Create Presentation" button in the center of the screen (You must have a gmail address that you can use)

6. On the Google presentation screen go to the upper left and click on "untitled presentation" and change the name—to make it faster to find your video change the name to the title of your video.

7. On the main navigaton bar select Insert > Video from the main menu

8. It will bring up a box that links to YouTube and from there you type in your video's title and your video should show up

9. Click on your video and say "add to presentation"— it will appear as a small thumbnail so drag out the sides to make it full screen

10. Go to the upper right corner and select publish/embed

11.	Click "Save & Close" in the upper right corner

12.	Go back to your LinkedIn Google presentation window, refresh the screen and your presentation should show up in the left window.

Select the presentation and click "Post to Profile"

You also have the option to "send to your network." You can promote the video to your Linkedin connections.

Promote videos via your blog

YouTube used to offer a setting to automatically upload your video to your blog, but they have since done away with this feature. You can, however still upload videos to your blog and/or blog site with the "embed" feature. To use the embed feature, first locate the video you would like to upload to the blog. Below the video you will see an embed button:

Make sure you link to your channel and your videos EVERYWHERE: The more links you have to a video, the higher it will rank when people are searching those keywords in YouTube or in Google or the other search engines. More links =more popularity=more traffic which helps promote your video, your brand and ultimately sales for you.

Video Chapter 8: Video Syndication and Strategy

The simple fact is that not everyone is on YouTube. There are other video sites that people use to find and watch videos. You want to make sure your message, and videos are out there in every way on every site possible. Also, you want to make sure your LINK to your website is visible everywhere to Google "spiders" when they are deciding which sites get to rank on the first page of searches. One of the easiest and FREE ways to do this is using a site like TubeMogul. TubeMogul allows you to take one video and syndicate it to many different sites.

It takes a few minutes to sign up for TubeMogul and each site you would like to syndicate to requires you to sign up for it individually but once you do this, it is SO easy, and did I mention FREE to get your video syndicated out to many different sites.

Make sure you use the principles and practices outlined in the previous chapters. Use your keywords and your URL in the video description, make sure you tag it properly and use original content.

The site TubeMogul has great tutorial videos that show exactly how you can use it. I highly recommend that you use a video syndication service, such as TubeMogul for maximum reach.

If you decide you want to submit to other video sites on your own be aware that not all sites are equal. Some appeal to certain demographic groups and others are flooded by specific types of content. The choice of video venue is important. YouTube, where millions of dreams and views come true, is the default host for any marketing video. However, because YouTube is the main video playground for millions of internet users, videos can get lost and forgotten without careful and dedicated SEO and marketing efforts. Other major sites have similar issues. Smaller sites promise less competition, but also have fewer viewers and may have questionable content.

Here are some strategies for video marketing to keep in mind:

1.   KISS -- Keep It Simple, Sir--A video must have something to say. Simple as this sounds, many marketing videos are too long and forget one of the most important things—the call to action! What do you want people who watch your video to DO? Make sure you ask them.

2. Think Hollywood--Although it is true that you don't need expertise to shoot videos for Youtube, no one wants to see your hand shaking or video of the ground a la "Blair Witch Project".

3.   Oversee and Analyze--Don't just release the video and forget about it, track the analytics, comments and subscriptions. Check your Google analytics to see if any traffic is coming to your website through your video marketing efforts. Make sure you pay attention to this venue as you would track a paper advertising campaign. Things like:

decipher performance by measuring conversion rates, demographics, entry and exit points, total views, etc.

4. Release Multiple Videos-- There is no perfect formula for video marketing. Each effort is a calculated gamble. As such, any video marketing strategy should never rely on a one-hit wonder. New content should be timely released to constantly feed viewer interest.

5. Integrate into Overall Plan-- Video marketing is only part of an entire online marketing strategy. It only reaches certain demographics, and is unable to convey detailed or extensive messages considering its limited time frame to capture attention. Videos should be integrated into the overall SMM strategy and networked with social media profiles, blogs, website, etc.

Suggested Weekly YouTube activity

- [ ] Make a list of videos and include topics such as how-to, lists and tips that you think would be of interest your audience.

- [ ] Check news sites and feeds to see if there are any relevant news stories circulating that you could use to add additional comments or content to create a new video post.

- [ ] Write a brief script, and practice—make sure each video is under 2 minutes. Make sure your call to action is in the first 10 seconds.

- [ ] Write the title, url descriptions, and tags in a word document so it can be easily cut and pasted when you upload the video

- [ ] Make a minimum of 1 video per week and syndicate it out using the method I have described.

- [ ] Search for videos you may find interesting and "favorite" those by clicking the little red heart near the video.

- [ ] Make sure your videos are uploaded to your other social networking accounts and to your blog

- [ ] Look at your page see if there are new subscribers or comments.

- [ ] If someone comments on your video, make sure you reply to their comments, thank them for viewing your video and contributing to the value by communicating with you.

- [ ] Engage with your viewers, ask them to rate your existing videos and give you suggestions on the future creations.

- [ ] Don't forget to ask them to engage with you on other social networks!

Final Thoughts

Do not underestimate the power of words and the speed with which information spreads these days. Be mindful of your message, bring value to your community and you will be successful in creating your PRESENCE, extending your REACH, increasing your VISIBILITY, growing your IMPACT and establishing your CREDIBILITY and EXPERTISE.

Make one of your goals this year to learn everything there is about Social Media Marketing for your business and start implementing what you learn. One of my favorite quotes is "Imperfect action is better than perfect inaction." Get started today!

SEO Checklist for Success

- ☐ Investigate and select your "niche" markets
- ☐ Do keyword research and write down your top 50 keywords
- ☐ Add your site to Google and other search engine's local listings using your keywords for better optimization.
- ☐ Optimize your site with keyword rich
  - ○ Title tags
  - ○ Meta keywords and descriptions for EVERY PAGE
- ☐ Write and install 250 word, keyword rich content with bolded keywords for maximum optimization
- ☐ Sign up for blogs, classifieds and a YouTube account to start building links
- ☐ Once per week write a minimum of 250 keyword rich blog content and post it on your blog
- ☐ Set up a Google Analytics account
- ☐ Install code on, at the very least, your homepage
- ☐ Set goals for traffic to your website
- ☐ Track your site stats weekly and tweak your site and your links accordingly.

Free Press Release Distribution Sites

Here is a list of some of the free press release sites I use (because these are free sites, they come and go quickly so test the links and use the ones that are best suited for you):

http://www.betanews.com
http://www.directionsmag.com
http://www.prleap.com/
http://news.thomasnet.com/
http://www.nanotech-now.com
http://www.prlog.org/
http://www.bizeurope.com/
http://www.free-press-release.com/
http://www.clickpress.com/
http://www.downloadjunction.com
http://www.newswiretoday.com/
http://www.openpr.com/
http://www.pressbox.co.uk/
http://www.filecluster.com/
htips://secure.digitalmediaonlineinc.com/
http://www.sbwire.com/
http://www.1888pressrelease.com/
http://www.afreego.com/
http://www.sanepr.com/
http://www.theopenpress.com/
http://www.free-press-release-center.info/

http://www.prfree.com/
http://www.ukprwire.com/
http://www.pressreleasespider.com/
http://pressabout.com/
http://www.pr-inside.com/
http://www.itbsoftware.com/
http://www.pressmethod.com/
http://www.itbinternet.com
http://www.newsblaster.com/
http://www.24-7pressrelease.com

List of Top Video Sites:

Blip.tv
BoFunk.com
eCorpTv.com
Dailymotion.com
Esnips.com
iviewtube.com
Kewego.com
MegaVideo.com
Metacafe.com
Myspace Videos
Photobucket.com
Revver.com
Spike.com
Ugoto.com
Veoh.com
Video.yahoo.com
vidilife.com
YouTube.com

Article Sites

Acmearticles.com
ArticleBiz.com
Articlecity.com
Articleclick.com
Articlecube.com
Articledepot.co.uk
Articlegarden.com
ArticlePros.com
Articler.com
Articlerich.com
ArticlesBase.com
Articlesnatch.com
Blogwidow.com
Goarticles.com
Homebiztools.com
Look-4it.com
Marketingarticlelibrary.com
Premierdirectory.org
reprintarticles.com
Searcharticles.net
Site-reference.com
Travelarticlelibrary.com
Ultimatearticledirectory.com
Upublish.info
Workoninternet.com

Directory Sites in order of Link Value

URL	Cost
DMOZ Directory - www. dmoz.org	Free
Yahoo Directory—www.dir.yahoo.com	$299/yr
Librarians' Internet Index -- www.ipl.org/	Free
Starting Point-- www.stpt.com/directory/	$99/yr
Business Directory--www.business.com/	$299/yr
Canny Link Directory -- www.cannylink.com/	$20
Americas Best Directory -www.americasbest.com/	$20
Joe Ant Directory- www.joeant.com/	$40
Chiff Directory- www.chiff.com/	$297/yr
Jayde Directory - www.jayde.com/	Free
Skaffe Directory www.skaffe.com/	$45
Ezilon Directory www.ezilon.com/	$199
Best of the Web Directory www.botw.org/	$299
Aviva Directory-- www.avivadirectory.com/	$150
Elib Directory--www.elib.org/	$90
V7N Directory--www.directory.v7n.com/	$50
RLRouse Directory--www.rlrouse.com/	$50
Gimpsy Directory--www.gimpsy.com/	$50
Go Guides Directory-- www.goguides.org/	$70
Qango Web Directory --www.qango.com/	$55
Big All Directory--www.bigall.com/	$15
Azoos Directory -- www.azoos.com/	$90
Clush Directory--www.clush.com/Dir	$20/yr
Illumirate Directory--www.illumirate.com/	Free
Business Seek Directory--www.businessseek.biz/	$20/yr
Internet Business Dir-- www.internetbusiness.co.uk/	$23

Other books by Kathryn Rose

Step by Step Guides to :
Facebook for Business
Twitter for Business
Linkedin for Business

The Parent's Guide to Facebook
Offers parents an in depth step by step guide to privacy and, including monitoring your children's online activities and how to protect them on Facebook.

The Tweens/Teens Guide to Facebook
Offers children the tools to help guide them through setting up and interacting on the world's largest social network with privacy and safety in mind.

The Grandparent's Guide to Facebook
Great for grandparents who want to keep in touch with their grandkids. Includes module on "Skype" a free service that allows free video and audio calls to stay connected.

Made in the USA
Charleston, SC
19 April 2012